Lighthouses England The South East

The lighthouses of Norfolk, Suffolk, Essex and Kent

Tony Denton and Nicholas Leach

▲ The old lighthouse at Dungeness.

◄ (Front cover) South Foreland lighthouse.

◄ (Frontispiece) The historic lighthouse at Lowestoft, the most easterly in England.

Published by
Foxglove Media
Foxglove House
Shute Hill
Lichfield
Staffordshire WS13 8DB
England
Tel (01543) 673594

British Library Cataloguing in Publication Data. A catalogue record for this book is available from the British Library.

ISBN 978-0-9513656-7-0

Layout and design by Nicholas Leach
Printed by Cromwell Press Group, Trowbridge

Contents

Lighthouse History

This book provides a comprehensive guide to the aids to navigation, lighthouses and harbour lights around the coast of East Anglia, the Thames Estuary and Kent, as well as inland lights in the Midlands. It starts at The Wash and ends with Dungeness on the Kent coast. These areas include some of the more famous and historically significant lighthouses in the British Isles, such as Cromer, Orfordness and North Foreland.

While the Corporation of Trinity House is responsible for many of these lights, including all the major ones, a number of significant small harbour lights are also in operation, and details of these have been included.

This introduction is intended to provide an overview of lighthouse history, development and organisation in England and Wales, focussing on the need for lights to mark the coasts of East Anglia, the Thames Estuary and Kent, and explain how Trinity House has developed into the service it is today.

The first lights

Trading by sea has been a principal activity of all civilisations, yet moving goods and cargoes by water involves facing difficulties and dangers such as storms and bad weather, avoiding reefs, headlands, sandbanks and cliffs, and making safe passage into ports and harbours. The need for aids to navigation is therefore as old as trading by sea itself, and today the major offshore lighthouses are supplemented by a plethora of small, locally-operated lights of varying sizes and range, which operate mainly around ports, harbours and estuaries to ensure vessels' safety.

The earliest aids to navigation were beacons or daymarks, sited near harbours or ports rather than on headlands or reefs, to help ships reach their destination safely. The earliest lighthouses were in the Mediterranean and the oldest such structure of which written records survive was that on the island of Pharos, off Alexandra, on the northern coast of Egypt. The Pharos lighthouse, that stood 466ft tall, was built between 283BC and 247BC and survived until 1326.

Perhaps surprisingly, the first navigational light to be shown along the coasts of Norfolk, Suffolk, Essex or Kent is almost as old. The Roman Pharos at Dover still survives in the grounds of Dover Castle. This structure was erected during the second half of the first century AD and was one of two lighthouses built on either side of the harbour.

The next lights to be exhibited specifically to help mariners were probably ecclesiastical ones, with several medieval coastal churches displaying lights of some kind. One of these was shown from St Edmund's Chapel, near Hunstanton on the north Norfolk coast, which marked the approaches to the port of King's Lynn and was maintained by a hermit. The hermitage of St Margaret's Strait, Kent, which is close to the site of the

present South Foreland light, was also probably associated with showing a light during the latter half of the seventeenth century.

As well as the ecclesiastical lights, privately-built and -funded lighthouses were erected at various locations before the industrial revolution took hold in Britain. The first recorded private proposal for a light was made in 1580 by Gawen Smith, but his intention of placing a beacon on the Goodwin Sands came to nothing. Another failed private application came in 1612 from John Allen of Rye, in Sussex, who wanted to build a lighthouse at Dungeness. Both he and subsequent applicants wanting to erect a light in this area failed due to lack of finance and the necessary influence with the Royal authorities.

A number of other early private lights were also built on the south-east coast. In 1614 a large number of local shipowners and masters petitioned Trinity House to consider a proposal

▲ The remains of the Roman Pharos lighthouse in the grounds of Dover Castle, next to St Mary's church, which was built in the late tenth or early eleventh century and reused much Roman brick in its construction.

◄◄ An engraving showing Dungeness lighthouse, 1690.

◄ The second lighthouse at Dungeness with its open coal fire. The amount of smoke gives an idea of the relative ineffectiveness of this form of light, and the difficulties which the keepers faced in maintaining it.

Lighthouse History

for a light displayed from the fifteenth century church tower at Winterton, but nothing came of this as it was stated that a light was not needed there. But at Orfordness and North and South Foreland, the soldier John Meldrum had more success. As one of the first lighthouse speculators, Meldrum, together with his associate Sir William Erskine, succeeded in obtaining a patent for Winterton in 1618.

The development of lighthouses around the coasts of the British Isles since then, during the last 300 years, has mirrored the development of trade routes. The nation's earliest lights were situated on the south and south-east coasts of England to aid vessels trading with France and north European ports. By the seventeenth century, however, the emphasis had changed, with lights built at strategic locations

on the east coast, as trade along the shipping lanes of the North Sea, primarily involving colliers taking coal from the industrial north-east and transporting it to London, had expanded.

During the eighteenth century statistics show that growth had been rapid, as tonnage registered in the capital expanded considerably. In 1700 about a third of all British tonnage afloat was registered in London, but a century later this had grown to two-fifths and was still expanding. The coastal trade at this time was dominated by the movement of coal from Newcastle and Sunderland, with forty per cent of coastal shipping in 1779-84 devoted to coal carriage, mainly to London.

The building of lighthouses in and around East Anglia, at places such as Cromer, Winterton and Orfordness, show the importance of the east coast trade route from the seventeenth century onwards. The Thames Estuary and Dover Strait were also important trading routes, and some of the earliest private lighthouses were built to mark these locations.

Trinity House

The organisation responsible for the operation and maintenance of the major aids to navigation today is the Corporation of Trinity House. The exact origins of Trinity House are obscure, but probably date back to the early thirteenth century, when groups of tradesmen, such as seamen, masters of merchant vessels and pilots, formed guilds to protect their interests.

One of the earliest such organisations was the Deptford Trinity House, which was incorporated by Royal Charter after its members had petitioned

◀ The tower at North Foreland as it was in the eighteenth century when owned by the Trustees of Greenwich Hospital. In 1832 it passed to Trinity House, which paid the Hospital £8,366 for this and the light at South Foreland.

Henry VIII to prohibit unqualified pilots on the Thames in 1513. Deptford was then a busy port and the main point of entry for the capital's trade, so pilotage duties were lucrative, and Trinity

◀ The present lighthouse at Lowestoft was built in 1870. Trinity House constructed their first lighthouse here in 1609.

Old Lighthouse Dungeness

PUBLISHED BY A. H. DE'ATH, ASHFORD.

The Lodge New Romney. July. 7th 1904.

▲ The lighthouse
built at Dungeness
in 1792 to the
design of Samuel
Wyatt, and pictured
shortly before its
demolition in 1904.
The keepers' houses
survive today.

Trinity House to build lighthouses on the East Anglian coast to guide vessels through the treacherous sandbanks between Happisburgh and Lowestoft. These ever-moving sandbanks took a high toll on shipping, so marking a safe passage through them was essential. To maintain the proposed lighthouses, a levy of twelve pence per ton was imposed on ships leaving the ports of Newcastle, Hull, Boston and King's Lynn.

However, despite the Crown's Orders, Trinity House was surprisingly reluctant to build lighthouses. The Corporation did build the tower at Lowestoft, the most easterly point in Britain, in 1609 and this is generally agreed to be the first they built. There is also evidence that the two towers at Caister, which Trinity House took over in 1607, had been built around 1600.

But instead of building lights themselves, the Corporation encouraged entrepreneurs to consider building them as profit-making undertakings. As a result,

House members wanted to retain their monopoly.

With losses of merchant shipping along the east coast trade routes to London becoming unacceptably high, a series of Orders in Council from the Crown, dating from the early seventeenth century, required

► South Foreland
lighthouse pictured
when in service.
This tower was
operational from
1843 to 1988,
and is now a
tourist attraction
maintained by the
National Trust.

private lighthouse ownership became relatively widespread during the seventeenth century, and the number of private lights increased during the following century as their erection and maintenance was left largely to private individuals.

Choosing the best position for a light, with sufficiently busy ports nearby from where revenue could be collected, was crucial for the light to yield a good return. Although a proliferation of unnecessary lights was prevented by the involvement of Trinity House, which had to grant permission for a lighthouse to be built, private light owners gained a reputation for greed, and lights were built around the coast on a somewhat haphazard basis. As a result, large areas remained unlit, and by the nineteenth century, with the level of trade increasing as industry grew, the situation had become unacceptable.

Trinity House had to accept the new demands for better aids to navigation, and, with the leases expiring on many private lighthouses, the Corporation was forced to take over. In 1807 Trinity House assumed responsibility of the Eddystone light off Plymouth, and the next three decades saw considerable changes to lighthouse organisation in England and Wales. In 1832 it bought out the towers at North and South Foreland, and gradually all the country's lights came under the Corporation's auspices.

These changes were formalised in 1836 with an Act

▲ An old postcard showing the high lighthouse at Dovercourt, one of a pair of iron lights which still stand and which helped to guide vessels into Harwich harbour.

of Parliament, which abolished privately-owned or leased lighthouses and gave Trinity House complete authority over all aids to navigation. The Corporation became the body to which others, including the regional Trinity House organisations, had to apply for sanction for the position and character of lights, as well as the alteration or laying down of new buoys. Although by this time most English lights were under the jurisdiction of Trinity House, the 1836 Act formally centralised lighthouse management.

The Act also gave the Corporation powers to use a compulsory purchase order on all privately-owned lights. Although only a few lighthouses were still in private ownership, the compensation paid to owners

Lighthouse History

cost the Corporation a staggering £1,182,546, and the fourteen towers in private hands in 1832 realised £79,676, almost the same amount as collected from the fifty-five towers under the control of Trinity House. The business of lighthouse operation had been a lucrative one for the individuals involved in it.

Just over a decade before the Act had been passed, in the 1820s, the leases on four private lights had been renewed by the government despite the recommendations of a Select Committee of 1822. These lights were at Harwich, Dungeness, the single patent for Winterton and Orford, and Hunstanton. All were extremely lucrative to their owners, and extricating them from private ownership proved to be far from straightforward.

The two towers at Harwich had been rebuilt in 1818 at a cost of £8,547 under a lease belonging to General Rebow. But the site was so lucrative that this amount was covered by the dues collected in just one year. At Dungeness as well as Winterton and Orford, the Lords of the Treasury initially decided to hand the leases to Trinity House when they ran out in the late 1820s, but then reversed these decisions after the owners, including Lord Braybrooke at Orford, had used their influence to persuade the Lords to change their minds.

Eventually, however, the private lighthouses were taken over, and by the end of the nineteenth century Trinity House had assumed control of lighthouse maintenance and construction. During the great period of lighthouse construction between 1870 and 1900, Victorian engineers and designers constructed and modernised at least fifty stations and built new rock towers. All of the

major lighthouses in East Anglia and Kent were modernised and improved, and some new stations were constructed, such as that at Southwold.

Harbour lights

Much of the literature about lighthouses has concentrated on the major lights, which are often impressive structures in spectacular locations. However, no less important are the many smaller lights found at most ports and harbours. They have developed in response to specific local circumstances, so their design, construction and purpose differ markedly, and the variety of such lights around England and Wales is considerable.

Many harbour authorities are responsible for their own aids to navigation, and this has led to a variety of lights and beacons being erected. Some ports, where vessels need to follow channels, have leading or range lights which, when aligned, mark a safe passage. Others have piers or breakwaters, the limits of which need marking, and on these some of the finest light towers have been constructed, such as that at Ramsgate.

The large harbour at Dover, now the country's busiest ferry port as well as a leading cruiseship port, has a number of aids to navigation, some in the form of significant lighthouses. In

▲ The lighthouse at Happisburgh, erected in 1790 as one of a pair, was built to mark a passage round the southern end of the notorious Haisborough Sands off East Anglia.

◄ The tower on the Isle of Grain, located behind the power station, overlooking the river Medway. The 66ft triangular structure is supported by piles and the quick flashing light is white, red or green. This structure is typical of the aids to navigation around the Thames and Medway estuaries.

Typical of the small harbour lights of the east coast is this now-demolished structure at Gorleston, marking the entrance to Great Yarmouth harbour. This old postcard shows herring drifters leaving harbour.

the Thames estuary, and the river itself, a series of lights guides vessels towards the capital, some of them quite significant structures. In areas where trade between ports was competitive, new harbours were built with grand lighthouses to mark their entrances. In areas where trade was more modest, smaller lights were erected, such as those at Lowestoft and Whitstable.

Lightkeepers

Throughout the history of lighthouses, the lightkeeper has played an essential role in maintaining the light. However, during the latter half of the twentieth century, the era of manned lighthouses came to an end as automation became

the norm for all operations. But before automation every light had to be manned.

The idealised view of lighthouse keepers conjures up a romantic image of men living in a tower with only the sea for company. While this was true for the remote rock stations such as Eddystone, where keepers were confined to fairly cramped quarters for weeks at a time, the reality for most keepers was a little different. The lights on the mainland had a senior keeper, who would be supported by two assistant keepers, usually with families. With automation, the lights can be controlled from a central location, and a locally-based attendant is responsible for general maintenance.

HRH The Duke of Edinburgh, Master of Trinity House, officiating at the ceremony at North Foreland as the keepers leave for the last time. This was the last lighthouse at which keepers served, and the last to be automated.

South East lighthouses

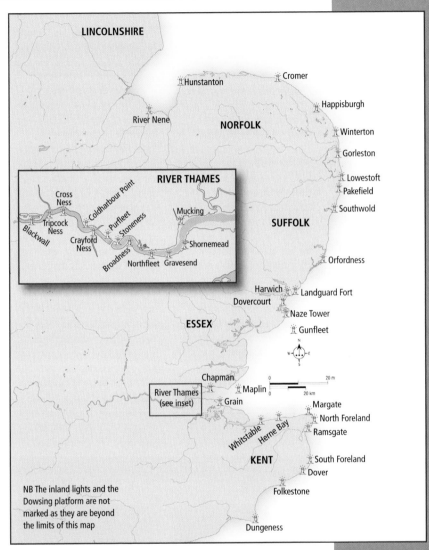

LINCOLNSHIRE

NORFOLK

Hunstanton
Cromer
Happisburgh
River Nene
Winterton
Gorleston
Lowestoft
Pakefield
Southwold

SUFFOLK

RIVER THAMES

Cross Ness
Coldharbour Point
Purfleet
Stoneness
Mucking
Tripcock Ness
Blackwall
Crayford Ness
Broadness
Northfleet Gravesend
Shornemead

Orfordness

Harwich
Dovercourt
Landguard Fort
Naze Tower

ESSEX

Gunfleet

Chapman
River Thames (see inset)
Maplin
Grain
Margate
North Foreland
Ramsgate
Whitstable
Herne Bay
South Foreland
Dover

KENT

Folkestone

Dungeness

NB The inland lights and the Dowsing platform are not marked as they are beyond the limits of this map

0   20 m
0   20 km

This guide to the lighthouses starts in the Midlands, with some unusual inland lights, then moves to the coast of Lincolnshire before running east and south through East Anglia, Essex and the Thames Estuary, ending with the lighthouses of Kent. The photographs show the lighthouses as they are today, and a number of historic images have also been included. The information about visiting the lights should be used only as a starting point. Consulting road atlases and Ordnance Survey maps first is advisable when visiting any of the locations.

Inland lights

CRICH STAND

ESTABLISHED
1855

CURRENT TOWER
1922

OPERATOR
Sherwood Foresters

ACCESS
The site and tower are open to the public with a car park at the site

There are reputedly only three structures in the British Isles that have displayed a light to guide travellers across treacherous land masses, and coincidentally they are all are in the East Midlands. Only two of these inland lights currently display some kind of light.

CRICH STAND • Crich is a large sprawling village on a hillside above the Derwent Valley, and one of its best-known attributes is its lighthouse, which is known as Crich Stand. It was built shortly after the end of the First World War above a quarry. The current tower is the latest in a long line of structures on Crich Hill, on whose summit the Romans probably had some kind of cairn or similar building on its summit. It was later said that a beacon was lit to signal the sighting of the Spanish Armada and another to celebrate victory. A beacon in a new brazier was lit in 1988 to mark the 400th anniversary of

the famous victory. It was rebuilt in the form of a cairn and brazier to commemorate The Queen's Golden Jubilee in 2002.

A wooden tower was erected in 1760 to mark the accession to the throne of King George III but lasted only twenty five years before being demolished. In 1788 Francis Hurt had a conical limestone tower with a wooden top built for £210, but this tower also fell into disrepair. Although it was rebuilt in 1849 from grit stone, some of the original stones were incorporated into its base.

The circular tower, which had a stone stairway up the inside and an inscribed tablet saying it was 955ft above sea level, was opened in 1855. In June 1882 a major landslip on the hillside weakened the base of the tower and, after later lightning storms, the tower was closed.

The tower could have just slowly decayed but in 1914 a relative of the original builder, also named Francis Hurt, sold an area of Crich Hill to the Clay

▶▶ The Crich Stand memorial honours those who gave their lives in both World Wars and subsequent conflicts.

▶ Crich Stand tower was built in 1922.

Inland lights

▼ Dunstan Pillar as it is today. The 1751 inscriptions on the sides of the tower can still be made out, albeit with some difficulty.

Cross Mining Company on the understanding that the tower, by then known as Crich Stand, would be demolished and rebuilt nearby. Because of the War, it was not until 1922 that the stones of the tower were removed and carefully labelled for future use.

In 1922 a memorial was erected to members of the Sherwood Foresters regiment who had fallen in the war. This coincided with the rebuilding of the original tower, which was then erected as a memorial to the regiment's soldiers using the original stone.

The Clay Cross Co donated the original stone plus £200, and agreed to transport all materials for the builder, Joseph Payne of Crich. The landowner Major F. C. A. Hurt of Alderwasley gave the land on generous terms. The architect Lieutenant Colonel Brewill died before the tower was completed in 1923, but his son completed the work. Built at a cost of £1,182 the 63ft circular tower was opened on 6 August 1923 and built into the tower is an original stone bearing the inscription FH1788.

The tower is topped by a domed stone lantern room in which a light was installed and first shown on 12 August 1934. It consisted of a 750,000 candle power twenty-eight-inch searchlight manufactured by Chance Brothers, which rotated eight times per minute and had a range of thirty eight miles. Although originally only shown on special occasions, it later shone every night. The light today is of less intensity.

DUNSTON PILLAR • In the 1700s, travellers making their way from Sleaford to Lincoln were often confronted by highwaymen on the heathlands of Dunston and Nocton. One such hold-up ended in the murder of Christopher Wilkinson. This incident occurred on land owned by Sir Francis Dashwood, who decided to make the road on the edge of his estate safer.

To this end, he decided to erect a land lighthouse which was tall enough for beams of light to be spread across extensive brush waste and thus deter highwaymen. The square stone pillar erected in 1751 was 92ft tall, and was topped by a gallery and an octagonal 15ft lantern, which was accessed by a spiral staircase inside the tower.

Although its purpose was to assist travellers at night, it soon became a tourist attraction, with amenities such as a bowling green and meeting rooms. As travelling conditions improved, the light was discontinued in 1788 and the lantern fell into disrepair. In 1808 it collapsed, and was replaced in 1809 by the Earl of Buckinghamshire with a bust made of Coade stone of King George III to celebrate fifty years of the King's reign.

In 1940 the tower was seen as a hazard to aircraft flying from the nearby Waddington Airfield, so the bust and thirty feet of tower were removed. The bust was displayed, somewhat damaged, in the grounds of Lincoln Castle until it was removed for restoration and returned to the pillar in 2008. There is a replica carving of the pillar and bust in the grounds of Dunston Village.

ST MARY'S, WELDON • The original name of the village was Weldon in the Woods, which gives a clue as to why a rather grand glazed cupola was erected on the tower of St Mary's Church in the village The story goes that a weary traveller, hopelessly lost in the hunting woods which in those days covered a large part of north-east Northamptonshire, eventually found his way by seeing the tower on the church. As a token of his gratitude, he provided a guide for other travellers by paying for a light on top of the tower. The light, which still shines each night, was encased in a fine cupola topped by a spire and a weathercock.

▲ The impressive cupola on the tower of St Mary's Church in Weldon, Northamptonshire.

◄ St Mary's Church in Weldon shows a light from its tower every night.

17

Dowsing

ESTABLISHED
Inner 1861
Outer 1873

CURRENT TOWER
Not existent,
discontinued 2003

OPERATOR
Trinity House

OUTER DOWSING • Just offshore to the south east of the Humber estuary are a series of sandbanks. They are the Haile Sand and Rosse Spit, with the long thin sandbank of Inner Dowsing Overfalls a little to the south. As early as 1861 Trinity House stationed a light vessel called Outer Dowsing at the northern end of this spit to guide ships both entering the Humber Estuary channel and travelling along the North Sea coast.

INNER DOWSING • In 1873 Trinity House positioned a light vessel at Inner Dowsing, slightly to the east and south of the original position. When the Outer Dowsing light vessel was withdrawn is not known, but it may be that this new vessel was in place of, rather than in addition to, that. In 1969 a second-hand platform, used by the National Coal Board and the largest drilling rig of its kind, became available so Trinity House purchased it and after a two-year refit towed it to Inner Dowsing, where it was sunk in position.

The rig was altered to include accommodation for three keepers below the main platform, which had a helipad and a service crane in addition to the 20ft red lattice tower with a gallery and lantern.

▶ The Inner Dowsing Light operated from this platform between 1971 and 1993.

This had been taken from Light Vessel No.87. The electrically-powered multicatoptric apparatus, which gave a white flashing light visible for twenty-four miles, was first displayed on 13 September 1971. This platform replaced one of the last Trinity House manned light vessels.

The Inner Dowsing platform was withdrawn in 1993. In 1994 the Inner Dowsing Light Vessel was re-established, but in 2003 it was again withdrawn. The last light vessel to serve at Inner Dowsing was LV 93, which was sold in 2004 and is now used as an artists' studio at Trinity Buoy Wharf, London, at Blackwall.

DOWSING B1D • During the 1950s a new hazard appeared in the form of rigs associated with the offshore gas fields, but with this hazard came an opportunity which Trinity House seized upon. They agreed with BP, the owners of the Amethyst Field, to erect an aid to navigation on the platform B1D, one of four in that field. Mounted directly on the rig itself, the light was equipped with four PRB 500 optics and a modern quartz Halogen light, giving a white flashing beam which was visible for twenty-two miles. Commissioned in 1991, this light was slightly to the north west of the Inner Dowsing platform.

ESTABLISHED	Inner 1950s
CURRENT TOWER	1950s
OPERATOR	Trinity House
ACCESS	No public access

◀ Lightvessel No.93 was the last vessel to serve at Inner Dowsing. It was deactivated in 2003, sold in September 2004, and now resides at Trinity Buoy Wharf, Blackwall, London.

River Nene

ESTABLISHED
1826 (possibly
never lit)

ACCESS
Although only about
100 yards apart as the
crow flies, the lights
are four miles apart
by road; the East
Lighthouse is situated
at the end of a narrow
road about two miles
from Sutton Bridge;
the West Light can be
approached via the
roundabout on the
west side of Sutton
Bridge into the village,
then the second left
down a winding road
passing King John
Farm and left to Guy's
Head; a footpath
passes close by

In 1826 the river Nene, where it emerged into the Wash, was realigned into what was then the new cut and what is now Nene Outfall. This level section from Sutton Bridge into the Wash was a fine new entrance and, to make it even more impressive, a pair of ornate lighthouses was constructed at the then headland. Since then land has been reclaimed and the towers are now a short distance inland.

These 60ft tapered towers are surmounted by an octagonal lantern with round windows and a single conical chimney protruding above the copper-clad roof. The East Light was a stand-alone tower, but buildings have been added as accommodation. Now a Wild Fowl Trust, it was occupied by the naturalist Sir Peter Scott during the 1930s.

The West Light, also known as Guy's Head Light, had a keeper's house attached, but it too has had more accommodation added. Although these lights were believed never to have been lit, in August 2005 the owner of the East lighthouse wrote: 'The lighthouses have and continue to have condensing lanterns lit automatically every night at the owners' expense.'

▶▶ The East Side lighthouse at the mouth of the river Nene, now in private hands having never operated as a light.

▶ Guy's Head lighthouse has been restored and is now in use as a private residence.

Hunstanton

ESTABLISHED
1665

CURRENT TOWER
1838-40

ACCESS
Near the Coastguard
lookout building on
the cliffs above the
beach

In 1665 two stone lighthouses were built at a cost of £210 on Hunstanton Cliff to mark a passage through the extensive sandbanks of the Wash. The lights had been built following the petitioning of King Charles II by shipowners who believed that the Old Lynn Channel needed marking to improve navigation. Shipowners paid dues of eight pence on every twenty tons of coal or other goods and one penny per ton was levied on foreign vessels to fund the light.

The inner light was coal-burning and the outer was fitted with candles. The former light had to be rebuilt after a devastating fire damaged it beyond repair towards the end of 1777. The new tower was 33ft in height, built of timber, and fitted with a reflector and oil lamps instead of an open brazier. The arrangement of the reflectors, designed by Ezekiel Walker, was such that a single oil lamp was set precisely in the focal centre, where the light rays would be set to their maximum intensity. The new light, shown for the first time in

1778, was more advanced and brighter than any lighthouse then in existence. It was the first time an illuminant other than coal was employed in a major light.

The tower remained in private hands until 1837, when Trinity House purchased the rights from the then owner, Frederick Lane. Plans were made for the timber structure to be replaced and in 1838 work commenced on a new circular brick tower. The tower, 63ft high from base to gallery, was constructed by William Candler, of King's Lynn, and showed a light for the first time on 3 September 1840.

In 1861 an additional floating light was established off the Lincolnshire coast at the Inner Dowsing Shoal, and in 1878 a light vessel was stationed at the Bar Flat. A chain of floating lights was gradually built up around the Wash, including the Dudgeon, Lynn Well and Roaring Middle light vessels. These combined to make the light at Hunstanton superfluous and so in 1921 it was discontinued and sold in 1922, when the lantern was removed.

▶▶ The disused tower at Hunstanton stands on the cliffs above the beach and has been converted into a holiday cottage , with the lantern replaced by an extra storey.

▶ Hunstanton lighthouse on the cliffs overlooking the beach, pictured when operational. It has been inactive as an aid to navigation since 1921 but was used as an observation post during the Second World War.

Cromer

▶▶ Cromer
lighthouse stands in
the middle of a golf
course to the south-
east of the town.

▼ The lighthouse,
built in 1833, with
the lantern used
before conversion to
electric operation
in 1958.

Before the lighthouse was built at Cromer, lights to guide vessels were shown from the tower of the parish church, which is one of the tallest in Norfolk, but this was not satisfactory. During the twenty years following the restoration of the monarchy in 1660, many proposals were put forward for lighthouses on all parts of the coast. One of the petitioners, Sir John Clayton, suggested that five lighthouses should be built along the east coast, including one at Foulness, to the south-west of Cromer, and another at Corton.

Despite facing opposition to his schemes, Clayton, together with George Blake, obtained a comprehensive patent in 1669, and at a cost of £3,000 erected towers at four sites. The patent was for sixty years and specified that dues be paid voluntarily by owners of passing vessels. But the cost of maintenance was high and, as many shipowners were unwilling to pay the dues, Clayton could not afford to kindle fires in the Cromer tower. However, despite being unlit, it served as a beacon and was marked on sea charts after 1680 with an explanation that it was 'a lighthouse but no fire kept in it'.

The owner of the land at Foulness, Nathaniel Life, considered that the situation required a lighthouse and took steps to light Clayton's original tower. Assisted by Edward Bowell, a Younger Brother of Trinity House, he persuaded the Brethren to apply for a patent. They obtained this in 1719, the dues to be a quarter of a penny per ton on general cargo and half a penny per chaldron (about twenty-five hundredweight) of Newcastle coal. Life and Bowell jointly received a lease, at a rental of £100 per annum, on the undertaking that the tower, together with the acre of land owned by Life on which it was

Cromer

▲ The lighthouse is adjacent to the Royal Cromer golf course. The current lantern, fitted in 1958, contains a third order catadioptric drum optic, which gives one flash every five seconds.

▶▶ The octagonal lighthouse, which stands about half a mile from the cliff edge, was converted to electric operation in 1958. The light is 275ft above high water and has a range of twenty-three nautical miles.

built, should pass to Trinity House when the patent expired after sixty-one years.

The coal-fired light was first lit and displayed on 29 September 1719, with the fire itself enclosed within a glazed lantern. Its ownership then passed through various hands during the eighteenth century, as both Life and Bowell died within twenty years of the light being first built.

Following a storm in October 1789, Trinity House pressed for improvements in all the local lights, and so Cromer was modernised and fitted with a new flashing light. This consisted of five reflectors with Argand lamps on each of the three faces of a revolving frame. The whole assembly turned one revolution in three minutes, giving a distinct flash and making Cromer then one of only two flashing lights.

The new light shone for the

first time on 8 September 1792, but the tower was under threat from the rapidly encroaching sea. In 1799, 1825 and 1852 huge sections of cliff slipped into the sea and the building was finally destroyed by a landslip in 1866.

The 1825 landslip showed that the lighthouse would eventually be the victim of such an event, so a new lighthouse was built, and this has served to the present. The white octagonal tower was completed in 1833 and exhibited a light twice as powerful as that on the tower it replaced. It was converted to electric operation in 1958 during a modernisation process that involved the complete removal of the lantern. In June 1990 the station was converted to automatic operation and the keepers' cottages became empty. They can now be rented as holiday accommodation.

Happisburgh

▶▶ The impressive
Happisburgh
lighthouse stands
just outside the
small village.

▼ There are ninety-
six stone steps on
the inside of the
tower's perimeter
wall which go to the
service room directly
below the light.

Happisburgh lighthouse, situated in the centre of a field about half a mile from the shore, is the oldest working light in East Anglia. It was established following a severe winter storm in 1789, when seventy sailing ships and 600 men were lost off the coast of Norfolk.

A subsequent inquiry drew attention to the lack of lights between Cromer and Winterton and resulted in Trinity House building two lighthouses at Happisburgh. A low light was erected on the cliff top, about 400 yards north of Cart Gap, and a high light, 85ft tall with the lantern 134ft above sea level, about 400 yards inland.

The two lighthouses, which replaced the old Caister lights, formed leading lights marking safe passage around the southern end of the treacherous Haisborough Sands. They were first exhibited on 1 January 1791. By keeping the lights in line, vessels were guided around the sands and into a sheltered stretch of water. In 1863, a new lantern was installed which consisted of diagonal frames crossing each other at a constant angle, enabling shipping to see the light from all angles to seaward. This remains atop the lighthouse.

The low light was discontinued in May 1883 after an extra light vessel had been stationed to guard the Haisborough Sands. Threatened by coastal erosion, the tower was demolished soon after it had been taken out of service. But with only one tower at Happisburgh, it was necessary to distinguish it from that at Winterton during daylight, and so in 1884 the Happisburgh tower was painted with three broad red bands, which remain today.

Happisburgh

The light was also changed to an occulting character, the light shining for twenty-five seconds followed by a five-second eclipse.

In 1929, acetylene was introduced, which meant the resident keepers were no longer needed, and the keepers' cottages were sold to become private dwellings. In 1947 electricity was installed, and the light, with a range of eighteen miles, was changed to emit a flashing sequence of three white flashes every thirty seconds.

In 1988 the future of the light came under threat when Trinity House undertook a major review of aids to navigation and included it in their list of five lighthouses and four light vessels to be discontinued. The date for scheduled closure and decommissioning by Trinity House was 13 June 1988. However, a petition to oppose the closure was organised, and the Friends of Happisburgh Lighthouse was established, funded by voluntary contributions, to promote the campaign. Trinity House agreed to postpone the closure.

Following an Act of Parliament passed in April 1990, the Friends were able to take control of the lighthouse after the Happisburgh Lighthouse Trust had been formally established as a Local Light Authority. The Trust is a registered charity governed by six trustees responsible for operating and maintaining the light, which became the only independently run lighthouse in the UK. The lighthouse has a character of three white flashes repeated every thirty seconds, with a range of eighteen miles. It is maintained and operated entirely by voluntary contributions.

Winterton

ESTABLISHED
1616

CURRENT TOWER
1840

DISCONTINUED
1921

ACCESS
Via the lighthouse holiday chalet complex

▶▶ The tower of the old lighthouse at Winterton which, together with the keepers' cottages, is now part of a private residence.

▼ The lighthouse has been inactive since the 1920s, while the keepers' cottages retain their distinctive look.

Winterton Ness was a notorious danger to shipping in the early 1600s, when it extended much further into Yarmouth Roads than it does today. Therefore Trinity House commissioned a pair of lights lit by candles at Caister to mark it.

However, the Brethren seemed reluctant to build a light at Winterton until, following a grant to John Meldrum to erect lights at Winterton Ness, they erected a tower in the village in June 1616. They were forced to relinquish control of the light the following April, after which Meldrum broke in and showed two candle-powered lights there from 1617. Following storms in the 1670s, Trinity Brethren erected a small front light in 1677, and so the area's two lights were operated by different bodies, each of which charged dues.

The changing shoreline meant the small light was relocated a number of times, but by 1683 the high light needed relocating. Sir Edward Turnour erected a new octagonal 70ft tower in 1685 and the Brethren built a small light in line; the lights were first kindled on 12 September 1687. In 1714 the front light was washed away and replaced. In 1791 following the erection of lights at Happisburgh, the Brethren discontinued the small light at Winterton. The high light was converted to oil with a glazed lantern and eleven reflectors.

In 1840 Trinity House replaced Edward Turnour's lighthouse with a new 62ft circular brick and masonry tower with a connecting keepers' dwelling. Initially lit by oil lamps, it was converted to a triple wick Argand burner with a prismatic lens in 1863. With the placing of offshore light floats, the light became redundant and was extinguished in the autumn of 1921.

Gorleston

ESTABLISHED
1878

CURRENT TOWER
1878

OPERATOR
Great Yarmouth Port
Authority

ACCESS
On Pier Road, situated
amongst shops on
the promenade at
Bush Bend, facing
the entrance to the
harbour; the pier is
open to the public

▶▶ The brick tower
at Gorleston is a
rear light for vessels
entering harbour.

▼ Gorleston
lighthouse situated
amongst shops on
the promenade, with
the leading light
in front facing the
harbour entrance.

The 69ft circular red brick tower in Pier Road opposite the harbour entrance at Gorleston was built in 1878. It has a gallery and lantern with a red conical roof. The lantern itself, which when operational showed a white light visible for six miles, is now unused. Today, a fixed red light, also visible for six miles, is displayed from the lantern room window. At a height of 23ft, an occulting white light is displayed through a first floor window, flashing four seconds on, two seconds off and visible for ten miles. This light is the rear light and works in conjunction with a front light mounted on a 19ft white metal pole on the roadside 115ft away. This white light, occulting every three seconds and visible for ten miles, is housed in a red cylindrical casing.

In 1852 a fixed white light was displayed on the south pier and, in 1887, a 30ft circular iron and wood lighthouse, complete with lantern and gallery, was erected on the end. This tower displayed a fixed white light in addition to red and green navigation lights. In 1902 a channel light was added, facing the harbour. When the pier was demolished in 1955, the tower was replaced by a series of lights fixed on the roof of the Harbour Master's office situated on the end of the new pier.

Performing a similar function to the original lighthouse, the lights are individually housed in metal and plastic lamp holders. Currently operated by the Gorleston port authority, EastPort UK, the main light gives a red flash every three seconds visible for eleven miles. A fog horn, of three blasts every sixty seconds, is also sited here. This building, near the end of the new south pier, is a 28ft high two-storey concrete and brick structure, and is now occupied by the National Coastwatch Institution.

Lowestoft

ESTABLISHED
1609

CURRENT TOWER
1874

AUTOMATED
1975

OPERATOR
Trinity House

ACCESS
On the east side
of the main A12
road into the town,
on a bluff behind
Lowestoft Ness, about
a mile north of the
harbour entrance

▶▶ The lighthouse
at Lowestoft was
built in 1874 at a
cost of £2,350 as
the High Light.

▶ The Low Light
at Lowestoft was
built of corrugated
iron on metal
legs and sited on
the promenade
immediately below
the High Light,
which can just be
made out to the left.
Built in 1867, the
45ft tower was a
movable structure. In
1923, the light was
made redundant and
demolished.

A pair of lights was first established on the low-lying foreshore of Lowestoft Ness in 1609 by the Brethren of Trinity House. The latticed timber structures supported candle lanterns and were known as Lowestoft High and Low lights. The towers stood in line, marking the deepest water of the Stamford Channel. To fund the lights, dues were payable at the rate of twelve pence per hundred tons on ships and four pence per voyage for fishing craft.

In 1628 the structures were found to be in a poor state of repair and so were rebuilt. The new towers lasted for a further fifty years until, in 1676, they had to be rebuilt again. The need for this was down to a number of factors: firstly, the towers had become hemmed in by fishermen's huts and dwellings, and the lights were partially obscured. Secondly, the lights had become more than a local inshore mark, which is what they were originally intended to

be, and had become useful to passing ships out at sea.

Thirdly, and perhaps most significantly, more powerful lights were needed not only as an aid to navigation but also to outshine the lights at Corton which John Clayton, a rival to the Trinity Brethren's monopoly, had erected. As a result, the High Light was moved to the cliff top on the north side of the town, its current location, so that it marked a safe approach through the Stamford Channel and also acted as a major coastwise light.

Throughout the rebuilding process, Samuel Pepys maintained a keen interest in affairs, having just become a Master of Trinity House. He was opposed to profiteering from light dues, and so was keen to see Lowestoft light in use, partly to prevent Clayton from making money from his tower. Work began early in September 1676, and by October the tower was ready, displaying a fire in place of the candles used hitherto.

Lowestoft

▶ The lighthouse at Lowestoft has changed little since it was built in the nineteenth century, although trams no longer run down what is the A12 road north of the town.

LOWESTOFT. THE LIGHTHOUSE.

▶▶ The lighthouse is situated above Sparrow's Nest and the local maritime museum to the north of the town, and is a major landmark on the Yarmouth Road.

The newly-rebuilt High Light, which still worked in conjunction with the Low Light, assumed the status of a major light and was visible for many miles along the coast. Meanwhile, the Low Light was discontinued in 1706, probably after having been washed away by heavy seas, and was not reinstated until 1730. A new timber structure was then built and a lantern displaying three oil lamps employed. The Low Light had to be rebuilt again in 1779 after it decayed, at which time the two lighthouses were classified as separate stations, each with its own keepers.

In 1796 both lights were converted to Argand lamps with parabolic reflectors. Before this, in 1778, a unique experiment using a light, described as the 'spangle light', was carried out at the High Light. The unusual mechanism consisted of a 7ft tall, 6ft diameter cylinder, with 4,000 small mirrors and 126 oil lamps. The light had a range of more than twenty miles but saw less than two decades of use.

In the 1870s it was decided by Trinity House that the High Light should be electrified, but the existing tower, which was almost two centuries old, was not strong enough to take the weight of the new equipment. As a result, work began on a new white cylindrical 53ft tower to replace the previous building in 1872, and it was completed in 1874. By then, paraffin oil was available as an illuminant and, as it was more economical and efficient, it was used in preference to electricity. Adjacent to the tower, accommodation for the keepers was built. The construction work was carried out by Suddelay & Stanford, of Beverley.

Both lighthouses were changed to coal gas from the town's mains in 1881, and the Low Light was discontinued in 1923, having been moved a number of times during the nineteenth century as the foreshore shifted. The High Light is still in service and today the light, automated in 1975, is visible for twenty-three miles.

Lowestoft Harbour

►► The light marking the end of Lowestoft's South Pier.

▼ The pier lights marking the entrance to Lowestoft harbour.

Lowestoft, the most easterly point on the English coast, developed from a small fishing village into a major port during the nineteenth century. The catalyst for this was the arrival of the famous railway contractor Sir Samuel Morton Peto in the 1840s, who constructed a railway from Lowestoft to Reedham, where it joined the Yarmouth to Norwich Railway. Together with other railways, it was operated by the Eastern Counties Railway.

After obtaining funding from the Norfolk Railway, Peto helped to develop the port, and moorings for about 1,000 boats were provided. In 1845 the port area was leased by the Norfolk Railway on an indefinite lease and the Eastern Counties Railway began work on building the dock system that still exists. By 1847 the two stone outer piers had been constructed, and a pair of lights was erected on their extremities to guide vessels into and out of harbour.

The port is currently managed by Associated British Ports, and their local personnel maintain both lights. They are white brick-built hexagonal towers, 39ft in height, with covered hexagonal aprons at the base forming bandstand type structures. The lights are housed in a domed roofed hexagonal lantern, mounted on a gallery accessed via an internal stairway. Known as Lowestoft North Pier and Lowestoft South Pier, they display lights with a range of eight miles.

The North light shows a green flash, four seconds on and one second off. The South light shows a red light with identical character; it also has a fog horn of four blasts every sixty seconds. At one time, this light structure was used as a pilot station.

Pakefield

ESTABLISHED
1832

DISCONTINUED
1864

ACCESS
On the cliff edge
adjacent to the
southern boundary
of Pakefield Hall
within the grounds
of Pontin's holiday
camp; the tower can
be accessed from the
beach or the land,
without entering the
holiday park

The 30ft white lighthouse at Pakefield was first lit in 1832, when it had a range of nine miles, but it had a comparatively short life. It was one of three subsidiary lights established within the vicinity of Lowestoft to try to accurately mark the changing channels offshore. The lighthouse at Pakefield was erected to mark the channel between the Barnard and Newcombe Sands.

A site was acquired in the grounds of Pakefield Hall on a low, sandy cliff, which was just over 30ft in height. A circular brick tower was constructed, surmounted by a lantern containing two Argand lamps. The lighthouse was built by James Taylor, of Yarmouth, at a cost of £821 9s 4d, having been designed by the London architect Richard Suter.

The light was displayed for the first time on 1 May 1832, and was a fixed red light visible for nine miles. By 1850, however, the channel it marked had shifted, so a light was erected three miles to the south at Kessingland. Once this was in operation, the Pakefield light was discontinued on 1 December 1864, at which point a pair of leading lights was set up at Hopton to mark the southern end of the Corton Sand, but these lasted only until 1871 and now no longer exist. The Kessingland light lasted until it too was extinguished in the early nineteenth century and no trace of it remains either.

Although no longer used, the Pakefield tower survived, and in 1929 it was sold to the owners of Pakefield Hall, which is now a Pontin's holiday camp. In 2000 a team of volunteers restored the tower, and the lantern room was given over to the National Coastwatch for use as a Coastwatch Centre, which is manned and open to the public during the summer.

▶▶ The lighthouse at Pakefield was built in 1832 and sold in 1929 to the owners of Pakefield Hall, which later became a holiday camp. The lighthouse is now surrounded by chalets.

▶ The tower has, since 2000, been in use as a Coastwatch station, having been renovated, and is open to the public.

Southwold

▶▶ Southwold
lighthouse has
a First Order
catadioptric
fixed lens.

▼ The lighthouse
has become one
of the town's
most prominent
landmarks.

The lighthouse standing in the middle of the small town of Southwold is a landmark for passing vessels, and guides craft into the town's harbour. The lighthouse is situated near the centre of the famous resort, at the highest spot in Southwold, nestling amongst rows of small houses in a picturesque setting. The site, beside the coastguard station, was described at the time of the lighthouse's building as 'very advantageous, the smoke from the town will not obscure the light and its nearness to the cliff must make it very prominent all along the coast'.

Construction of the 101ft tower began in May 1889 under the supervision of Sir James Douglass, Engineer-in-Chief to Trinity House. The impetus for building this light was accelerated by the low light at Orfordness being washed away. Following this, on 19 February 1889 a light was displayed from a temporary wooden structure on Southwold Denes.

Once completed, the new lighthouse came into operation on 3 September 1890. It was originally provided with an Argand burner, but this was replaced by a Matthews incandescent oil burner in 1906. A Hood petroleum vapour burner was installed in 1923 and remained until the station was electrified in 1938, when the keepers were withdrawn and the station de-manned. The tower first shone as a flashing light on 23 February 1938.

Two red sector lights, with a range of fifteen nautical miles, mark shoals to the north and Sizewell Bank to the south, while the main navigation light is white with a range of fifteen miles. A locally-based attendant visits the lighthouse regularly to carry out routine maintenance.

Orfordness

Orfordness lighthouse, situated at the end of a thirteen-mile spit running parallel to the Suffolk coast, was formed by centuries of longshore drift. The dangers of the tides, banks and shoals in the area have claimed many ships. On one night alone in 1627, thirty-two ships were wrecked on Orfordness with few crew members surviving.

In February 1634 John Meldrum was granted a patent, which later passed to Alderman Gore, to build two temporary lights to mark a safe passage through the gap between the Sizewell Bank and Aldeburgh Napes. Under a further patent granted during the reign of Charles II, Gore built two timber towers, the high rear light to burn coal, and the lower front light to exhibit a candle lantern.

Ownership passed to Sir Edward Turnour via marriage to Sarah Gore, and he secured his position by acquiring the land on which the lighthouse stood, as well as a large area of Lantern Marshes to provide access to the site. But under Turnour and, after his death in 1676, his son, another Edward, the lights were badly maintained, and complaints were often made by masters of passing vessels.

In 1691 the encroaching sea carried away the low light. It was duly replaced, only to be again carried away by the sea in 1709. In 1720 the lighthouses came into the ownership of Henry Grey, who organised the building of two new brick towers for £1,180. Four years later, the front light was destroyed by erosion, and so it was replaced by a movable structure. Between 1730 and 1790 two more towers had to be built to replace structures that had burnt down.

In 1792 a new 98ft brick tower was built by Lord Braybrooke, who had inherited ownership. Situated much further inland from the point of the headland, it became the great light, and the previous great light then became the small light. This brick tower, designed by the architect William Wilkins, the son

▶▶ The current Orfordness dates from 1793 and, on 6 July 1964, became the first light to be remotely controlled from Harwich.

▶ The lighthouse with keepers' houses on both sides of the tower. These buildings were later removed.

The Lighthouse - Orford. No 6.

Orfordness

▶▶ The red and white painted lighthouse at Orfordness is situated at the end of a thirteen-mile spit which runs parallel to the coast.

▼ The Orfordness lighthouse pictured before 1959, when the keepers' dwellings either side of the tower were demolished.

of a Norwich plasterer, and first lit on 6 May 1793, has become the operational light.

Under the Act of Parliament of 1836 which gave Trinity House compulsory powers to buy out private individuals who owned lighthouses, the Corporation paid the third Lord Braybrooke £13,414 for the lighthouse. In 1888 major alterations took place at the great light, or high light, which was made occulting with red and green shades fitted to form sector lights. At the same time, the lower tower was taken out of use and a new light established at Southwold.

Further alterations were made in 1914, when a new revolving lens was installed which is still in operation. It revolves around the lamp at a speed which appears as a flash every five seconds, with a range of twenty-five nautical miles. When this light was installed, a subsidiary light was fixed halfway up the tower to act as the colour sector light.

In 1959 the lighthouse was converted to electric power, backed up by stand-by generating facilities, and the keepers' dwellings, which were attached on either side of the tower, were demolished. A stand-by generator was then installed, followed by remote control equipment. Time switches came into operation, the station became fully automatic on 6 July 1965 and on 20 September 1965 the keepers were withdrawn. At this time the main navigation light was a 3KW 100V filament lamp. New equipment was subsequently installed in the form of a 1KW 240V Mercury Vapour Discharge lamp.

Trinity House still maintains the lighthouse, which is over 200 years old and has survived raids by privateers, storms, machine-gun fire and flying-bombs. When first built, it was 1,439 yards from the front lighthouse, and hence the sea, but recent coastal erosion means that the site is threatened, and the future of the tower is under consideration. During very low spring tides, the remains of the brick foundations of the low light lost in 1887 are uncovered.

Felixstowe

ESTABLISHED
1841

DISCONTINUED
1925

ACCESS
None of the small
navigation lights at
the Port of Felixstowe
is accessible, and
nothing can be seen
from the land

The shifting sandbanks and movement of the tip of Landguard Point made entry into the river Stour, and thence to the ports of Ipswich, Harwich and Felixstowe, difficult for vessels. The main hazard was Andrews Shoal, which extended halfway across the river from Landguard Point. To help vessels negotiate the river entrance, in 1841 a temporary light was displayed from Landguard Fort on the north side showing a white, red and green light. This was replaced by a permanent light on Landguard Point in 1861.

The permanent light was shown from a 38ft white wooden tower on stilts located near the tip of the point. The lower eight-legged portion was open, with an enclosed service area just below a balcony. The fixed red and white light was in a circular lantern above, adjoining the keeper's house, which consisted of a small oblong bungalow with a pitched roof. This light, which was visible for five miles, was destroyed by fire in 1925 and never replaced, as light buoys were considered sufficient to guide vessels up the river and to the various ports.

The lights on Landguard Spit were primarily to assist vessels into Harwich, as Felixstowe had its own navigation lights, consisting of a pair of red range lights for mid-channel, on South Entrance East Pier and Felixstowe Pier. The lights were realigned by 8ft in 1903 and in 1910 the pier light on the grain silo was changed from red to white. With the rapid expansion of Felixstowe in the twentieth century into one of the country's main container ports, these lights have been replaced by lights on each wharf, none of which is accessible.

▼ The lighthouse at Landguard Point marked the entrance to the river Stour until destroyed by fire in 1925.

Harwich

In 1665 two lighthouses were built in Harwich to guide ships through the entrance to the river Stour. The High Light was situated in the centre of the town, in what is now West Street, with the Low Light on what is now the promenade. The lights had been erected by Sir William Batten, one of the principal officers of the Navy Board, who had successfully petitioned parliament. But somewhat surprisingly, Trinity House allowed a patent for a lighthouse to fall into the hands of a speculator rather than build one themselves.

However, the lights were described as 'two feeble and inefficient lights on two makeshift structures totally unsuitable for the purpose'. The low light was situated 200 yards from the high light and was shown from a crude 22ft wooden tower on which was displayed a single candle which was raised and lowered daily.

After a succession of renewals to Batten's patent, General Francis Slater Rebow was given a new grant in 1816 with the proviso that he not only improve the lights under the supervision of Trinity House but contribute sixty per cent of his profits to the upkeep of the church and local street lighting. In 1818, on the original sites, he built the two lighthouses which are still standing, converting the High Light from coal and the Low Light from candle power to Argand lamps and reflectors.

The lights were displayed at the same height as the old ones, but realigned by 9ft to the south-west. The High Light was a 70ft nine-sided brick tower with a pinnacle roof. A brick chimney extended above the roof on the landward side. Initially the

▼ The 1818-built Low Light at Harwich, now the local maritime museum, with Felixstowe Container Terminal in the background.

Harwich

white light, consisting of nine oil burners and reflectors, was shown through a window 40 feet below the top with the top section used as a land mark.

Despite the change to the Low Light in 1819, the lights were still ineffective, due to the fact that the height differential was too little. The light was therefore moved up by 25ft to a window near the top in 1822, and the illumination was increased to ten burners, which gave it a range of thirteen miles. This solved the problem, and the light remained in this arrangement until being discontinued later in the century.

The Low Light is an ornate octagonal pagoda type tower, on top of a brick shelter. Painted white, both the shelter and tower have a black roof. The light, which consisted of three oil burners and reflectors, was shown through a window 5ft below the top. After complaints,

the light was changed in 1819 from white to red to help distinguish it from the High Light.

The lights were taken over by Trinity House in 1837, but both were discontinued in 1863, when the continuing build-up of Landguard Spit rendered them ineffective in accurately marking the channel into the river.

Both of the towers were sold to Harwich Town Council in 1909, and had to be kept available for possible future use as lights if necessary. The High Light was partially restored in 1974 and then, when leased to the National Vintage Wireless and Television Trust in 1991, completely restored. It is now open daily as a museum. The Low Light was, from 1970 to 1974, reclaimed by Trinity House as a pilot station. Now fully restored, it has been used as the Harwich Society Museum since 1980 and is also open to the public.

Dovercourt

ESTABLISHED
1863

CURRENT TOWER
1863

DISCONTINUED
1917

OPERATOR
Harwich Town Council

ACCESS
On the sea front at
Dovercourt

▶▶ Dovercourt
High Light on the
beach, near the
promenade. In
2005, both lights
were leased to Tony
O'Neil, who planned
to open the High
Light as a museum.

▼ Dovercourt Low
Light stands a little
way offshore from
the High Light.

Between 1862 and 1863 a pair of lights was erected at Dovercourt to replace the Harwich lights to the north after they had become ineffective due to a changing of channels and the build-up of Landguard Spit. Both lights were erected on movable structures to enable them to be realigned if necessary.

The 45ft High Light at Dovercourt, adjacent to the promenade, was a black-painted six-sided metal cast-iron tower supporting a white wooden lantern with black roof. An external ladder led to the first level, with an internal stairway from the accommodation block to the balcony and lantern. The 27ft low light was an eight-sided structure mounted on four legs. It was 200 yards to sea and could be approached by a causeway at low half tide. Lit by gas, the lights provided a way mark for ships entering the new channel into Harwich, with the High Light visible for eleven miles and the Low Light for nine.

The accommodation in both lighthouses was practically identical with a small entrance hall, a staircase to the lantern, a living room with a cooking stove, a bedroom with bunks and a flush toilet. Water and town gas were laid on, with telephones in both lighthouses.

They were discontinued in 1917 and in 1922 sold by Trinity House to Harwich Town Council on the understanding that the lights would be demolished if they became unsafe. Both lights, now no longer movable, were restored between 1983 and 1988 by the High Stewards Lighthouse Appeal and are now listed historic structures.

Naze Tower

CONSTRUCTED
1720

OPERATOR
Privately owned

ACCESS
For a small charge the Tower can be visited; it is usually open between 1 April and 1 November; for more information see nazetower.co.uk

Naze Tower, situated to the north of Walton-on-the-Naze, near Walton Hall, was constructed in 1720 by Trinity House and, when lined up with Walton Hall, guided ships through the Goldmer Gap in the nearby shoals. However, there is some doubt whether and for how long the tower actually displayed an aid to navigation. If it was lit, a brazier on top with an open fire must have been used initially.

Information about its exact height is contradictory, with some records stating it was originally 90ft tall and others 86ft. Constructed of red brick, the tower was octagonal, in three sections, each of which was slightly narrower than the lower one. At the base it was 18ft 6in wide, and buttresses ran the full height, with the top castellated. Access was via an internal spiral staircase, which was illuminated by arched windows.

During the nineteenth century the top was rebuilt and reinforcing was added. At this time the tower was slightly reduced in height, creating doubt as to whether it is now 81ft or 86ft tall. Whichever it is, this grade II listed building is the tallest such structure in the British Isles.

The tower has had a variety of uses. During the eighteenth century, when tea was an expensive commodity, the Rt Hon Richard Rigby MP, owner of Walton Hall, used the tower to house exclusive tea parties. A century ago it was used as a signal station by the Royal Navy, who adorned it with signal flags to communicate with other signal stations and ships. During the Second World War the Royal Air Force used it to house radar operators and a Chain Home Low Radar Dish was fitted on the roof.

Despite these activities, the tower deteriorated, until it was placed on the Buildings at Risk register. This resulted in a local family carrying out work on its full restoration in 2004 and, as a result, the tower was opened to the public as a tourist attraction. The highlight of the climb, via 110 steps, is the rooftop viewing gallery, which offers panoramic views over Essex and, on a clear day, as far as Kent.

▶▶ Naze Tower can be seen north of Walton and it now houses, situated over eight floors up, a tea room as well as a museum, art gallery and shop.

▶ The Naze Tower overlooks the Essex coast and is now a popular spot with visitors.

56

Gunfleet

ESTABLISHED
1850

DISCONTINUED
1920

OPERATOR
Gunfleet Sands
Offshore Windfarm

ACCESS
Only via boat

▼ The Gunfleet
lighthouse has been
in existence for over
150 years, but is
now semi-derelict.

Gunfleet lighthouse is one of the few screw pile structures that survives. It was erected in 1850 to mark the north entry into the Thames and the Gunfleet Sands, six miles off Clacton-on-Sea. The 74ft screw pile tower consisted of six outer piles and a single central pile driven into the unstable sand base.

Designed by Mr Walker of Trinity House and based on an idea by the blind Irish engineer Alexander Mitchell, the lighthouse itself consisted of a red-painted hexagonal corrugated iron accommodation block, with the light mounted in a small lantern on top. The submerged end of each pile had a broad-bladed screw, which was twisted into the sandy bottom. The platform was then constructed on top. The revolving white light, visible for ten miles, was supplemented by a fog bell.

In 1920 the tower was decommissioned and replaced by a buoy. Although unoccupied since, it was sound enough to be used by the pirate radio station Radio Atlantis. In September 1974 they had the light structure made safe, with windows cut and floors installed so that a generator could be installed, with a studio and transmitter on the upper floor and accommodation below. But as the light is situated at the northern extremity of the Port of London, it was just inside territorial waters, which enabled the Home Office to remove the equipment on 26 November 1974. On 19 December 1974 those involved returned to the structure to be met by Marines, the Essex Police and Trinity House officials, who persuaded them to abandon the project without it ever transmitting.

In 2002 meteorological equipment was installed in the tower as part of research into a proposed windfarm on the sands. In 2009 work commenced on the installation of forty-eight wind turbines on the Gunfleet sands, which will change the area's appearance over the next twenty years. Today the structure, although neglected, remains in remarkably good condition and stands as a daymark surrounded by bell buoys marking the treacherous sands.

Thames Estuary

Ships approaching the lower reaches of the Thames were guided by a number of manned lighthouses which now no longer exist. Some were built on sandbanks on the Essex side of the estuary, and details of these are as follows.

MAPLIN • The lighthouse on the Maplin Sands was unique. It was built in 1838 through the efforts of a blind Irish engineer, Alexander Mitchell, who, in 1833, obtained a patent for a screw pile lighthouse. Five years later, he constructed one on Maplin Sands, the first in the world. Designed to sit on sandy or muddy seabeds, it relied on 4ft diameter screws on the end of five-inch diameter solid cast-iron piles to provide a firm base for the upper structure. At 69ft tall and 50ft in diameter, the Maplin light consisted of eight outer piles and a single central one to support an octagonal service area with the optic showing a flashing white light in a circular lantern on top.

It is claimed that the screw pile lighthouse in the river Wyre off Fleetwood was the first in the world and the first to show a light, but Maplin's screw piles were in fact in place before those at Fleetwood. When the West Swin moved its flow northwards, the lighthouse was undermined and in 1932 was swept away.

In recent years, the southern edge of the sandbank has been marked by two light beacons, Blacktail East and Blacktail West. Built in 1968, the 42ft towers, constructed of mild steel, show isophase green lights visible for six miles. Initially battery-powered, they were for a time powered by experimental wind generators until converted to solar power in 1996. The lights are offshore and visiting them is not viable.

CHAPMAN • Situated on Chapman Sands near Canvey Island, Chapman lighthouse was erected in 1849. A screw pile lighthouse designed by James

MAPLIN

ESTABLISHED
1838

DISCONTINUED
1932

▼ The Maplin lighthouse as depicted in an old hand-coloured postcard.

Thames Estuary

Walker for Trinity House, the 74ft structure was supported on six outer piles and one central cast-iron pile, had a red-painted accommodation block, consisting of a living room, bedroom, kitchen/washroom and storeroom with a lantern above, and displayed a fixed white light visible for eleven miles. It was later altered to an occulting light.

During the two World Wars it was used as a marker for convoys leaving the Thames as they awaited an escort, but in the 1950s ut was undermined by the sea. In 1956 it was demanned, and during 1957 and 1958 demolished. A single black

buoy is now used, situated 800 yards offshore.

MUCKING • On the eastern part of Mucking Flats, where Sea Reach gives way to The Lower Hope, a screw pile lighthouse, similar to that at Chapman, was erected in 1851. Initially it was a 66ft black and white tower, but was raised to 70ft and painted red in 1881. Unlike Chapman, where the keepers had to row ashore, the light at Mucking was connected to land by a long footbridge which was supported by screw piles.

The original coal-fuelled light showed a white occulting light

► The lighthouse erected in 1849 on the Chapman Sands near Canvey Island; the structure was demolished just over a century later.

with a red sector and was visible for eleven miles. It was replaced by the No.1 Mucking Buoy before the Second World War. As a result of the 1953 floods on the riverbed, and after being hit by the barge Anglia, the lighthouse was removed in December 1954.

PURFLEET • An experimental lighthouse with attached dwelling was built in 1829 on Beacon Hill, overlooking the Thames at Purfleet, to enable Trinity House to carry out experiments to determine the effectiveness of different lamps and reflectors. Different fuel sources were also tried, and the merits of reflectors and refractors, with different grades of glass, were evaluated. The lighthouse was only used infrequently and was abandoned in the late 1870s. Due to quarry working, it was totally destroyed in 1925.

▲ Two somewhat indistinct views of Mucking lighthouse and the walkway which joined it to the shoreline.

◄ A line drawing of the now-demolished light at Purfleet overlooking the Thames.

River Thames

Nine land-based lights are in operation on the Thames, and would be accurately described as unattended light structures rather than lighthouses. Erected and maintained originally by Trinity House, they were taken over in 1991 by the Port of London Authority (PLA), which is responsible for one of the busiest ports in the country.

In total, the PLA maintains sixty-six aids to navigation, and the land-based lights represent only a small percentage of the total navigation marks on the river. The following descriptions cover the lights in geographical order, starting on the Essex side, going west along the north bank, then east along the south bank.

STONENESS • Situated where the river bends into Long Reach, the Stoneness light was built in 1885. The 42ft square skeleton tower has a service room just below the lantern which shows a green flashing light visible

for six miles. The tower and lantern are red, with the service room white. A wind generator was mounted on top to supply the light after it was converted from acetylene to electricity. It is possible to get reasonably close by walking the coast path across Thurrock Marshes.

COLDHARBOUR POINT • Coldharbour Point light, located near Rainham Marshes, marks the bend between Erith Rands and Erith Reach. It was built to a standard design in 1885 and consists of a red 39ft lattice steel skeleton tower with a gallery and light on top. Access to the lamp, which shows a flashing white light visible for three miles, is via an external ladder. A footpath and track lead to this isolated light, but the whole area is essentially a landfill site.

TRIPCOCK NESS • Outward bound on the southern side of the river, the first light is situated at the east end of Gallions Reach

► Coldharbour Point marks the bend in the Thames between Erith Rands and Erith Reach.

►► Stoneness light on the south bank of the river Thames, close to the M25 Dartford River Crossing.

River Thames

▲ Tripcock Ness light is on the south side of the Thames

at Tripcock Ness. Built in 1902 to a similar red lattice steel design as Coldharbour, the 30ft tower shows a flashing white light visible for eight miles and is surrounded by a red palisade fence and razor wire. Access is easiest by taking the coast path or the cycle track along the top of the flood defence embankment from Thamesmead Leisure Centre.

CROSS NESS • At the east end of Barking Reach is Cross Ness, where another standard-design lattice steel light tower was built in 1895. The 41ft tower displays a flashing white light visible for eight miles. It is surrounded by a palisade fence and situated in a

housing estate. It is accessible via the estate or by walking along the river from the leisure centre.

CRAYFORD NESS • At the east end of Erith Rand, where it gives way to Long Reach, is an unspectacular light at Crayford Ness. It was originally a stone-built structure erected in 1946 to the landward side of the sea defences in an industrial area. The stone tower was replaced by a standard red lattice steel tower in 1967.

This tower was demolished in 1981, when the flood defences were improved, and now the light is housed in a corrugated iron shed halfway up the smaller, at 74ft, of the two Port of London radar towers on the embankment. These two towers are connected by a walkway from the top of the lighthouse tower. Two lights are shown through a window, one flashing white, visible for eight miles, and the other fixed white, visible for three miles. As with the other lights, this one can be approached via the coast path or the cycle track on the embankment.

▶ Cross Ness or Leather Bottle Point light stands in front of a housing development at Thamesmead.

BROADNESS • At Broadness, where the river takes a sharp bend from St Clement's Reach into Northfleet Hope, is a simple light mounted on a 43ft tripod connected to the land by a walkway. It was erected in 1975 to replace the previous standard lattice tower dating from 1885. Converted to electricity in 1981, the occulting red light is visible for twelve miles. The light is difficult to visit, as public footpaths across Swanscombe Marshes stop some way short.

NORTHFLEET • At the bend where Northfleet Hope gives way to Gravesend Reach, Trinity House established their first Thames light in 1859 on India Arms Wharf, at Northfleet, to guide inward-bound ships. A 53ft four-legged skeleton tower, it differs from the other lights in that it has a gallery and a lantern with the light shining through a window. The occulting light had both red and white sectors visible for fourteen and seventeen miles respectively.

The red-painted tower had three circular equipment balconies mounted in stages up the tower. It was fuelled by acetylene, and later converted to town gas, before being changed to electricity in 1975. This light was called Northfleet Lower after a second light, Northfleet Upper, was erected in 1926 on the Associated Portland Cement Company's jetty. The black and later white 27ft skeleton tower was demolished in 1972 and replaced by a light, still operational, on top of an eight-storey semi-derelict office block

▲ The light at Crayford Ness is mounted halfway up the smaller of these two radio communication towers.

◀ The light at Broadness, joined to the riverbank by a walkway with the container cranes at Tilbury in the background.

on Bevans Wharf a few yards from the lower light. Northfleet Lower was discontinued in about 2001 and its duties passed to Northfleet Upper.

SHORNEMEAD • Situated about two miles east of Gravesend, on the junction between Shorne Marshes and Higham Marshes, where Gravesend Reach gives way to the Lower Hope, is Shornemead light, also known as 'the Parson's Light'. The area's first light was erected in 1913 and consisted of a 48ft red cylindrical metal tower mounted on timber piles. It was connected to the land by a metal walkway, which was gradually extended to overcome river erosion.

By 2003 the light itself had been undermined and was leaning, and so it was replaced by a modern 50ft tower. The new tower consists of a red and white circular tube with three galleries, each accessed via an external ladder. The flashing light is displayed from the upper one and has white, red and green sectors visible for seventeen, thirteen and thirteen miles respectively. The old light was fuelled by acetylene until converted to mains electricity. The new light, which is not connected to the land, is powered by solar panels

◣▶ The operational light at Northfleet is mounted on top of a disused office block on Bevans Wharf, adjacent to the original light.

▲ The now defunct Northfleet Lower light, which was built in 1883 on India Arms Wharf.

▶ The modern functional light at Shornemead dates from 2003.

mounted on the top gallery. The light can be seen from the Saxon Shore Way footpath. Since being replaced, the old light has been stored at Denton Wharf, which is inaccessible to the public.

GRAVESEND • Gravesend, on the south shore of the Thames Estuary, has no fewer than three piers, Town Pier, Royal Terrace Pier, and a commercial terminal with jetties. Both the Town and Royal Terrace Piers have small aids to navigation. The Royal Terrace Pier was built in 1844 and the tower has an open cupola-style lantern rising from a single-storey pier building. The lantern is white and the continuous red light that is displayed has a focal plane of almost 50ft.

◀▲ The base on which the tower at Shornemead was built in 1913.

▲ The Shornemead light of 1913 at Denton Wharf.

◀ The light at the end of the Royal Terrace Pier at Gravesend. The pier is used by the PLA workboats and the lifeboats.

Blackwall

ESTABLISHED
1854 as experimental
lighthouse

CURRENT TOWER
1864

OPERATOR
Docklands
Development
Corporation

ACCESS
The site at Orchard
Place, Blackwall, is
open to the public, the
tower by arrangement

Before keepers were sent to lighthouses they needed to be trained in their duties, and so a squat square building in London Docklands was built as a training facility. Trinity House set up repair and maintenance workshops on the north side of the Thames adjacent to Bow Creek in Orchard Place, Blackwall, in 1804. They also repaired lightships there, so in 1822 they realigned and strengthened the river bank.

In 1854 an experimental lighthouse, designed by James Walker, was constructed at the site to test different forms of illumination. In 1863-64 the depot was completely rebuilt and a second lighthouse, the one seen today, designed by Sir James Douglass, was erected alongside the first. The lights were never used as aids to navigation.

The physicist Michael Faraday spent time here developing his ideas. Between 1836 and 1865 he was scientific adviser to Trinity House, and he set up a laboratory at Blackwall. He oversaw the programme to electrify lighthouses, and also conducted experiments into electrochemistry and electrophysics. Prince Albert arranged for Faraday the use of a grace and favour house at Hampton Court from 1858. Faraday spent increasing amounts of time there in the 1860s and, following his death, was buried in the Sandemanian plot in Highgate Cemetery.

In the late 1920s the original lighthouse was demolished, but the current lighthouse continued to be used to test lights and train keepers until 1988.

This lighthouse, attached to the depot buildings, is a hexagonal tower about 35ft tall topped by a gallery and lantern. The top of the lantern was shaped in such a way as to expel the exhaust gases from experiments with different fuels. The light source and optic were changed according to the training or experimental exercise.

During the Second World War the lightship activity was transferred to Harwich, but the workshops, which were damaged in German bombing raids, were repaired. The repair and maintenance activities were therefore continued until 1988, when Trinity House transferred them to a state-of-the-art purpose-built depot at Harwich.

The Blackwall Depot is now owned by Docklands Development Corporation and the area, including the lighthouse which looks over Greenwich and the Millennium Dome, is managed by Trinity Buoy Space Management as a site for arts and cultural activities.

What had been a hidden corner of London Docklands has become a thriving centre with artists' studios and galleries and, most recently, the opening of the University of East London's new Fine Art studios. The most striking aspect is the brightly coloured Container City. This studio and office complex, made from recycled sea shipping containers was featured on Channel 4's televsion design programme, Grand Designs.

▶▶ The brick hexagonal tower lighthouse, with a traditional light and workshops, situated on Trinity Buoy Wharf on the Thames opposite the London Millennium Dome. Built in 1863 by Trinity House, this light was used for training purposes and was part of training and workshop facilities operated on this wharf. The site became redundant in 1988.

Herne Bay

ESTABLISHED
Unknown

CURRENT TOWER
Unknown

OPERATOR
Unknown

ACCESS
There is no public access but can be viewed from promenade

Herne Bay came into prominence during the late Victorian era as a seaside resort. It has never been a port, but the tower of Herne Church was reputedly maintained as a lighthouse for three centuries and the fire basket remains stored in the top chamber of the tower.

During the mid-nineteenth century excursion steamers ran regularly from Herne Bay, calling from Margate and Ramsgate. A pier was built to enable passengers to board, and a quick flashing light was mounted in an octagonal lantern on a 49ft concrete building on concrete piles in the pier's centre section.

However, most of the pier was demolished by the Army as a counter-invasion measure at the start of the Second World War and the landward end and seaward terminal are now separated by half a mile of water. The remaining dilapidated seaward section of the pier still supports this small light.

Seafront regeneration in the 1990s saw the creation of a sea defence jetty to protect low-lying areas of the town which were subject to flooding. This concrete jetty, known as Neptune's Arm, has created a small harbour used by working and leisure boats. At its end is a small leading light.

▶ The small light at Cartwright Point, the name given to the end of the modern breakwater.

GRAIN • Another small light on the north coast of Kent is that at Grain on the Medway, which is a triangular 69ft lattice steel triangular tower. Situated on the river bank to the east of the power station, the tower has a gallery but no lantern. The quick flashing light has white, red and green sectors visible for thirteen, seven and eight miles respectively. The road through Grain village provides access to it (see page 11 for photograph).

▶ The light at Herne Bay was halfway along the longest pier in the UK, but the pier has slowly fallen into the sea and all that remains is this section from which a light is displayed.

Whitstable

On 3 May 1830, two years before the port of Whitstable was officially opened, the railway line from Canterbury, known as the 'Crab and Winkle' line, was completed. When the harbour was opened on 19 March 1832 the line's terminus was on the East Pier. To assist vessels, which were mainly colliers bringing coke for the ovens, enter the narrow harbour entrance, a pair of leading lights was erected on the 50ft white-painted brick chimney of the engine house.

A fixed red light visible for five miles, which indicated when the harbour was closed, was placed in a polished copper lantern on a balcony at a height of 40ft. A fixed white light, visible for nine miles, was mounted in another copper lantern on a 5ft high tripod on top of the chimney. Originally oil-fired, the lights were subsequently converted to electricity. Once the chimney was made redundant after the Second World War, the light was placed on top of the smokeless stack. An iron steeplejack ladder was bolted externally to the stack for the local lamp man to use in order to refill and service the lamps.

During the early twentieth century the harbour fell into disrepair, and in 1958 was purchased by the Borough Council. As part of the Council's redevelopment during the 1960s, the buildings on the East Quay, including the chimney and its lights, were demolished. When the East Quay was reopened in 1965, the original lanterns had been taken for display in the Whitstable Museum and Gallery.

Now, the only light is a small aid to navigation on top of a metal pole on the East Quay to guide the ships and small vessels that use the port, and no sign of the old lights remains.

ESTABLISHED
1830

DISCONTINUED
1950s

OPERATOR
Local port authority

▼ The lighthouse of 1830, amongst buildings on the East Quay at Whitstable, was demolished in the late 1950s.

353   QUAY AND LIGHTHOUSE, WHITSTABLE

Margate

ESTABLISHED
1828

CURRENT TOWER
1954

OPERATOR
Thanet District Council

ACCESS
Can be seen from
the promenade and
reached by walking
along the jetty

The Royal Harbour of Margate was formed by the construction of an impressive 900ft-long stone pier in 1828. There had been a pier at Margate since the sixteenth century, although it was destroyed several times. But in 1808 John Rennie, a leading civil engineer of the day, recommended the construction of a substantial protective breakwater, and stone from the old pier was incorporated into the structure which, together with stone brought from Whitby, formed the new harbour.

A lighthouse was constructed at the head of the pier in 1829. The tower was a Doric column, 100ft in height, which supported a light in a cast-iron lantern accessed via an internal spiral staircase. Built by Rennie and Jessop to the design of a Mr Edwards, it was topped by a weather vane, and stood as a local landmark until destroyed by the gale and floods on 31 January 1953 during what became an infamous storm.

During the rebuilding work after the storm, the light was replaced in 1954 by a new 66ft hexagonal stone tower, which is still standing in the same location and which was designed by W. R. H. Gardner FRIBA. Built by Dorman Long & Co, the tower displays a continuous red light, which is visible for three miles and is housed in a lantern with gallery. The lighthouse, mounted on a broad base, is a prominent local landmark and can be seen from the promenade.

The pier, which is owned by Margate Pier & Jetty Company, has a plaque describing the light's construction as well as one which reads: 'In commemoration of the landing at Margate Jetty of 46,772 troops of the Allied Forces on the evacuation of Dunkirk in May 1940.'

▶▶ The lighthouse at Margate, built in 1954, is situated at the end of the pier, which dates from the nineteenth century.

▼ Margate harbour with the original lighthouse of 1828.

North Foreland

On Kent's north-eastern corner, on the outskirts of Broadstairs, stands the impressive North Foreland lighthouse, which plays an important role in marking the Margate Roads and helping ships which are entering or leaving the Thames and passing through the Dover Strait. It has a significant place in the history of Trinity House as it was one of the first to come under the Corporation's management, and the last station to be manned.

A navigation light was reputedly displayed at the site as early as 1499, although it was probably not lit continuously and was more likely to have been used to warn of attack or piracy than as an aid to navigation. It was more a beacon than a light, and was initially wood-fired in an iron basket, which was hoisted up and down using a lever, or 'swape'. This was later replaced by a lantern on a pole supporting twenty-four candles.

The next light at the Foreland was built after Sir John Meldrum had obtained a patent from Charles I to place lights at both North and South Foreland and charge ships passing between the two. Although Meldrum was opposed by Trinity House, which argued that this would be an unacceptable expense on shipping, a tower was built of wood after he had been issued with a patent on 13 February 1637. This allowed him to maintain fires at both North and South Foreland for fifty years at a rent of £20 a year, payable to the Crown. To recoup his costs, he was permitted to levy a due of one penny per ton on passing ships. The tower he erected burned to the ground in 1683.

Following a period when a temporary candle-powered light was used, a new 39ft flint and brick octagonal tower was erected in 1691 supporting a coal fire basket. In 1719 both North and South Foreland lights passed by will to the Trustees of the Royal Naval Hospital at Greenwich, and thus under the indirect management of the Royal Navy. The brick foundations

▶▶ North Foreland lighthouse and associated buildings is one of the best-known lighthouses in Britain. The keepers' cottages are now holiday lets administered by Rural Retreats on behalf of Trinity House.

▶ An old postcard of North Foreland when it was manned and the keepers' cottages were occupied.

NORTH FORELAND LIGHTHOUSE BROADSTAIRS

North Foreland

were extended to create an impressive tower.

From about 1728 to 1730 the light was enclosed in a lantern, but this proved unsuccessful, as soot and smoke obscured the light, so the open fire was reverted to. In 1793 the tower was increased in height by two storeys to improve its range, and a new lens, designed by Thomas Rogers and revolutionary at the time, was fitted. However, this was not a total success and was replaced in 1834. By then, the station had come under Trinity House control having, in 1832, become one of the first

lighthouses taken over by the Corporation during the expansion of the nineteenth century.

In 1866 the tower was modernised, rendered and painted white. The keepers' accommodation was moved from the tower to two purpose-built keepers' cottages joined to the tower by a short passage. The lantern on top contained a multi-wick burner and first order catadioptric fixed lens, which is still in place, although it was converted to electricity in 1920. The white flashing light, which has two red sectors, is visible for nineteen miles.

▶ North Foreland lighthouse in the 1960s. It had been modernised in 1866 to the design of James Walker, Engineer-in-Chief to Trinity House, and his alterations gave it the appearance that it retains today.

During the 1990s the station was an area control centre and the keepers were responsible for light vessels in the Dover Strait and other land-based lights. However, the extra work this entailed for the keepers did not last long, as the station itself was automated. When the keepers left on 26 November 1998, North Foreland had the distinction of being the last lighthouse to be automated. A ceremony, attended by Prince Philip, was held to mark the occasion.

Since then, the keepers' cottages have become holiday homes for letting, while the lighthouse itself was opened to the public by the East Kent Maritime Trust in 2000. It is open to visitors at weekends from Easter to September, with extra openings in July and August.

▲ The lighthouse at North Foreland stands in immaculately kept grounds and shows a white light with a range of nineteen nautical miles, along with two red sector lights of sixteen and fifteen nautical miles respectively.

◀ The lighthouse seen from the air, showing some of the houses built on nearby land at the edge of the town of Broadstairs.

Ramsgate

►► The lighthouse at Ramsgate was built to the designs of John Smeaton.

▼ The lighthouse on the West pier of Ramsgate harbour seen from the sea.

Although Ramsgate has been an important landing site since medieval times, work on the construction of a harbour did not commence until 1749, and it was not until 1779 that the East and West stone piers were constructed to form the outer harbour. In 1783 John Smeaton drew up plans for a lighthouse on the end of the West pier, but he died in 1792 without completing the project. However, the lighthouse was eventually built in 1795 by Samuel Wyatt, and consisted of a 34ft circular tower of Cornish granite on a granite base. The light was displayed in a lantern room with a gallery.

In 1842 it was decided to replace this tower with a 38ft circular stone lighthouse set a short way back from the end of the pier. Operating as a rear range light, it now shows a fixed red light visible for four miles when less than 10ft of water is in the harbour, and a fixed green light at other times. The lantern is painted red and has an ornate roof. The front range light is mounted on a 13ft red and white pole on the end of the East pier and shows a white occulting light visible for four miles.

Two rock breakwaters extend from the harbour, on the end of which are two 30ft cylindrical towers each carrying solar-powered lights. The North Breakwater has a green and white banded tower with a quick flashing green light, and the South Breakwater tower has red and white banding with a red light. Ramsgate harbour has the distinction of being the only Royal Harbour which was given Royal status by King George IV in recognition of the hospitality given to him when he sailed from Ramsgate to Hanover.

South Foreland

Although a navigation light at South Foreland was recorded as early as 1367, details of it are sketchy. Reputedly, a hermit living in a cave in a nearby village used to light a beacon fire. However, it was not until 1636 that a lighthouse was built on the cliffs overlooking St Margaret's Bay to warn shipping of the dangers of the notorious Goodwin Sands.

Its construction followed a legal wrangle which resulted in Sir John Meldrum obtaining a patent to place lights at both North and South Foreland and charge ships passing between the two. Meldrum built two lights at South Foreland, one well back from the cliffs, and the other 230ft from the cliff edge which, when aligned, marked the treacherous Goodwin Sands. Built of wood and plaster, the towers housed open fires in fire baskets.

From about 1719 to 1730, the lights were enclosed in a lantern, but this proved unsuccessful, as the lights were obscured by deposits on the glass from the smoke, and so they were returned to open fires. The lights were enclosed again in 1793, when they were converted to sperm oil lamps with reflectors, and the towers were rebuilt and improved at the same time.

When Trinity House took over the station in the 1830s, the Brethren decided to rebuild it to their own plans. The high light was rebuilt in 1843 by James Walker to a typical Trinity House design, with two attached stone dwellings joined by short corridors to the 69ft octagonal stone tower. The optic was enclosed in a circular lantern with a stone gallery. The low light was also rebuilt, 1,000ft nearer the cliff edge than the main light, and in an easterly direction, in 1846 to a similar design. The total cost of the rebuild, including new optics, was £4,409 4s 3d. The two lights worked together so that when a ship's navigator lined the lights up vertically a safe passage past the Goodwin Sands was marked.

The lighthouse is well known for the many experiments carried out there and, in December 1858, it was the first to show an electric light using Professor Holmes's magneto-electric lamp followed

▶▶ The picturesque octagonal lighthouse at South Foreland, decommissioned in 1988, is now owned by the National Trust and stands on the famous White Cliffs, near St Margaret's-at-Cliffe.

▶ The South Foreland low light built by Trinity House in 1843 was 1,000ft nearer the cliff edge than the high light.

South Foreland

▶▶ South Foreland lighthouse, from the air, is a prominent landmark on the famous white cliffs of Dover.

▼ The lighthouse today operates as a tourist attraction. It ceased to be operational in 1988 and is now a National Trust property.

by Dr Siemens's dynamo. In 1873 the main light was converted to electricity, and sirens and gunshots were also tested as fog signals over several years. Perhaps the most important experiment was carried out by Marconi on Christmas Eve 1898, when he successfully spoke by radio to the Goodwin Sands light vessel. This was the first two-way ship-to-shore radio message to be exchanged

In 1904 the low light was discontinued, as the continually shifting sands meant that the safe passage once marked by the lights now went directly over the sands. The high light, which stood only 49ft above the ground but 374ft above sea level, was then transformed from a fixed light to a rotating first order Fresnel lens with its flashing beam visible for twenty-six miles.

The lighthouse was decommissioned in 1988 and then sold to the National Trust, who maintain the building and open it up for visitors. The lens and its rotating mechanism were removed, but in 2000 it was returned to the station. Soldiers of the First Parachute Regiment carried the mechanism up the tower's winding staircase so that it can be seen by visitors today. A tour of the tower includes the lantern, service room, engine room and unique weight tube.

Having been decommissioned in 1904, the low light has been left empty ever since. The 49ft stone tower and empty lantern room still exist in a private garden not accessible to the public, but are now almost derelict, while the keepers' dwellings that were attached to the tower no long exist.

Dover

ESTABLISHED
AD40-120 (Pharos Tower)

CURRENT TOWER
1902, 1909, 1987

OPERATOR
Dover Harbour Board

ACCESS
Admiralty Pier can be walked after payment of a small fee; Prince of Wales Pier is open to the public; neither breakwater light is accessible

▶▶ The Prince of Wales Pier Light in Dover harbour was built in 1902.

▼ The lighthouse on Admiralty Pier dates from 1908 and is at the end of the 4,000ft pier.

From the time the Romans were in Britain, lighthouses were in use to guide ships into the port of Dubris, the Roman name for the town. Some time between about AD 40 and AD 120 the Romans built two fortified octagonal rubblestone towers, known as the Eastern and Western Pharos, on the cliffs either side of the harbour. The western tower is now just a small mound, known locally as the Brendon Stone. Part of the eastern tower, however, stands within Dover Castle and at 46ft is the tallest Roman ruin in Britain. It was originally an eight-storey 80ft tower with an open fire on top, but only three storeys now survive, with part of a fourth.

The modern port of Dover was developed during the nineteenth century, although it had been a safe refuge before then, and was indeed the chief Cinque Port. But the Duke of Wellington was concerned at the inadequacy of the defences on the coast, so in 1842 insisted that a harbour of refuge be built. During the construction of the new harbour, a lighthouse was erected on the end of the North Pier in 1842 and on the South Pier in 1852. Between 1854 and 1864 the South Pier was extended by 1,000ft and renamed Admiralty Pier, and between 1871 and 1875 it was extended by a further 300ft. In 1899 work started on extending the 2,000ft long Admiralty Pier to form the new Admiralty Harbour, and by 1900 it was completed to its current length of 4,140ft. All of these various piers were marked by their own lighthouses.

In 1908 a lighthouse was erected on the end of the new extension. The light was shown from a white round 72ft conical cast-iron structure, complete with a lantern and gallery, displaying

Dover

▶▶ The lights at the end of Admiralty Pier and, nearest camera, the western end of Dover Breakwater, which together mark the western entrance into Dover harbour.

▼ The Breakwater Knuckle light is situated on the breakwater which forms the outer limits of Dover harbour.

a flashing white light which is visible for twenty miles. During this work, the South Pier light was demolished.

While the Admiralty Harbour was under construction, a new pier, initially called East Pier but then the Prince of Wales Pier after the Prince laid the foundation stone on 1843, was built to replace the North Pier. The pier was completed in 1902, and at its end a lighthouse was erected. This was a 46ft circular stone tower with a white lantern and gallery, which now displays a quick flashing green light visible for four miles. This lighthouse is the only stone tower in the harbour, as the other three are

cast-iron structures. In 1987 the infamous hurricane caused severe damage to the lighthouse, which was rebuilt and resited to its current location.

Two lighthouses were erected on the southern breakwater when it was built in 1909. The Southern Breakwater West Head, a 73ft cast-iron circular tapered tower with a white lantern and gallery, shows an occulting red light inside the harbour, and a white light outside the harbour every thirty seconds, which is visible for eighteen miles. This light was not shown between 1940 and 1960, as the western harbour entrance was blocked for military purposes.

On the knuckle, a further white circular cast-iron lighthouse, known as Harbour Knuckle Light, was erected in the same year. This 52ft tower stands on a square stone base and has a similar lantern and gallery. Its flashing light, visible for thirteen miles, also shows red inside the harbour and white outside.

Although the eastern entrance into the harbour was completed in 1909 with the construction of the Eastern Arm and Southern Breakwater, no lighthouses were built to guard it. Today a set of red and green traffic lights are used to control the arrivals and departures of the many vessels, and a similar set is installed alongside the Admiralty Pier lighthouse at the western entrance. The eastern entrance is used exclusively by ferry traffic, with other vessels moving through the western entrance.

Folkestone

▶▶ The lighthouse
at the end of the
pier is now called
Folkestone Harbour
Breakwater Head.

▼ The original light
at Folkestone pier,
built in 1848, was
in existence for
almost a century.

Up to the nineteenth century Folkestone was a small fishing village whose shingle beaches made it very difficult for boats to land on the shore, so a pier and harbour were built, with work lasting from 1807 to 1820. However, sand and silt choked the harbour, and removing it was costly. When the South Eastern Railway Company took over the harbour in 1842, they commenced dredging the harbour, and the town became the Company's principal station for traffic to the continent.

One of the Company's first acts was to erect a rather ornate white-painted 41ft square wooden lighthouse on the end of the old harbour pier in 1848. In addition to a white flashing light visible for thirteen miles, it had a square observation post on top. This light, called Horn Tower lighthouse, was decommissioned and removed in 1941 to make way for a gun emplacement.

Their next move was to build a new breakwater in 1860, which was extended in 1874 to improve the harbour, and then further expanded between 1881 and 1883. A lighthouse was built on the end of this breakwater in 1860, when the breakwater was constructed. This new light was a slightly tapering 28ft circular stone tower with a white-painted lantern room and gallery, and a light showing two white flashes every ten seconds, visible for twelve miles, and increased to every two seconds in fog. It also has a fog horn giving four blasts every sixty seconds.

The lighthouse has become accessible since the harbour area was purchased and redeveloped by Roger De Haan in a partnership with Sea Street Project in 2005. A walkway was constructed to give access to the lighthouse, which may be replaced by what planners describe as an 'iconic lighthouse'.

Dungeness

ESTABLISHED
1615

CURRENT TOWER
1961

AUTOMATED
1991

OPERATOR
Trinity House

ACCESS
The sites can be easily visited and the 1904 lighthouse, now in private hands, is open to the public during the summer season

Dungeness is a vast expanse of shingle ridges, built up by centuries of longshore drift. By the seventeenth century it was sticking out into the English Channel and become a dangerous hazard to shipping. Many ships have been wrecked in the area, particularly as the spire of nearby Lydd church once caused confusion to sailors. During one winter gale over 1,000 sailors lost their lives, along with much valuable cargo.

The first lighthouse to mark the spit dates from August 1615, when Sir Edward Howard obtained a patent from King James I and erected a light near the tip. Initially coal-fired, it failed to pay its way, as dues proved difficult to collect. Howard sold the licence to William Lamplough, who succeeded in collecting dues via the Customs House at nearby ports to fund the light.

Although the light was converted to candle power, it was criticised by Trinity House as being unhelpful to navigation in the area, possibly because the shingle bank had grown since its construction, and so

in 1635 Lamplough replaced it with a 110ft wooden tower, with keepers' quarters, nearer the sea. He also reverted to an open coal grate but, due to the ever-shifting shingle, the sea gradually moved further from the light and complaints were again made about its inadequacy.

Trinity House insisted it be resited, so in 1792, funded by the Earl of Leicester, Samuel Wyatt built a 116ft stone tower similar in design to Smeaton's Eddystone. The new tower was 100 yards from the shoreline. The light was provided by seventeen Argon lamps, which were fuelled by sperm oil, and was magnified by silvered concave reflectors.

In 1836 Trinity House, empowered by Act of Parliament, bought out all lighthouse leases, including that at Dungeness. They continued to maintain the light and in 1862 pioneered commercial electricity by introducing it to power the light at Dungeness on an experimental basis. The electric power supply, however, was then in its infancy and this trial proved too costly, so the station reverted to an

▶▶ The black painted lighthouse at Dungeness built in 1904 and decommissioned in 1961.

▶ A mid-nineteenth century engraving of the 1792 tower which lasted for more than a century.

Dungeness

oil light. The new oil lamp was surrounded by more effective and much-improved glass prisms.

However, as the shingle bank continued to expand, by the late nineteenth century the tower was about 400 yards from the shore. Trinity House therefore placed a movable low light on the end of the spit and the existing tower became the high light. Also oil-fired, the low light showed a very quick flash. By the turn of the century, however, the high light was even further from the sea so, in 1904, it was demolished. In its place a new tower, now known as Dungeness Old Light, was erected between 1901 and 1904.

At 143ft in height, the Old Light is one of the tallest lighthouses in Britain. Built of brick by Pattrick & Co, with a lantern and gallery, it was originally painted with broad black and white bands, but is now all black. The revolving lens gave a white flashing light with red sub light visible for eighteen miles. At the same time, the movable low light was replaced by a static white cast-iron circular tower on top of a white oblong brick fog signal building 400 yards from the high light.

When the nuclear power station was built, it obstructed the light and so the tower had to be replaced. A 131ft circular concrete tower, impregnated with bands of black and white pigment, was erected, housing a fog signal just below the lantern. The tower was equipped with xenon electric arc lamps, but these were not a success and were replaced by an array of sealed beam units which had a range of twenty-seven miles.

In 2000 the lighthouse was refurbished and a revolving optic was installed with a reduced range of twenty-one miles. The tower is floodlit at night both as an additional guide to shipping and to reduce bird losses.

▶▶ The current lighthouse at Dungeness was built in 1961; the tower is 131ft in height.

▼ The circular keepers' building built round the base of the 1792 tower remains between the two existing lighthouses, with the early twentieth century keepers' cottages also still in existence.

Glossary

Acetylene A highly combustible gas which burns with an intensely bright flame.

Argand lamps A bright and relatively clean-burning lamp invented by Francois-Pierre Ami Argand in 1783.

Automated An unmanned light controlled externally; all the major UK lighthouses are automated, with Trinity House controlling and monitoring its lights from the Corporation's Depot in Harwich.

Beacon A structure, usually land-based, either lit or unlit, used to guide mariners.

Character The identifying feature of a lighthouse is its character; for example the light could be described as fixed, or flashing.

Daymark Light towers often also serve as daymarks, which are fixed unlit beacons visible from the sea and marking a navigational hazard.

Dioptric lens A development by Augustin Fresnel consisting of a bull's eye lens surrounded by a series of concentric glass prisms. Dioptric lenses were classified by the focal length.

Elevation The elevation refers to a light's height above sea level; the higher the elevation, the greater the range.

Flashing light A light where the period of light is less than the period of darkness.

Fog signals A sound signal, often located with a light, used to warn mariners in times of fog or heavy weather.

Gallery The external walkway encircling the lantern.

High light The taller or higher of a pair of lights.

Isophase light A light where the periods of light and dark are equal.

Keepers The persons responsible for maintaining and keeping the light, as well as the associated buildings, at an aid to navigation.

Lanby The abbreviated term for Large Automatic Navigation Buoy, a modern floating unmanned aid to navigation often used in place of a lightship.

Lanterns The glass-enclosed space at the top of a lighthouse housing the lens or optic; lanterns are often encircled by a narrow walkway called the gallery.

Lightship A vessel, powered or unpowered, designed to support a navigational aid.

Low Light The shorter or lower of the two lights used to mark a channel or hazard.

Occulting Where the period a light is exhibited is greater than its period of eclipse; this can be achieved in several different ways.

Range lights Lights in pairs which mark a channel.

Reflector A system which intensifies light by reflecting the light source into a beam, both to increase intensity and to enable the beam to be manipulated to produce differing light characteristics.

Training wall A bank or wall erected below water level in a river or harbour mouth to train the water flow.

Bibliography

Hague, Douglas B. and Christie, Rosemary: Lighthouses: Their Architecture, History and Archaeology (Gomer Press, Dyfed, 1975).

Jackson, Derrick: Lighthouses of England and Wales (David & Charles, Newton Abbot, 1975)

Long, Neville: Lights of East Anglia (Terence Dalton, Lavenham, Suffolk, 1983).

Medlicott, Gordon: Discovering Lighthouses: A tour of discovery along the coast of East Anglia (2000).

Medlicott, Gordon: Discovering Lighthouses: A tour of discovery along the coast of Kent (2000).

Nicholson, Christopher: Rock Lighthouses of Britain (Patrick Stephens, Somerset, 1995).

Woodman, Richard and Wilson, Jane: The Lighthouses of Trinity House (Thomas Reed Publications, 2002).

Websites

www.alk.org.uk Association of Lighthouse Keepers; unique archive, a museum at Hurst Castle, quarterly Journal, field events; registered charity.

www.lighthousedepot.com Comprehensive list of world lights with details, photos, locations and links.

www.trabas.de/enindex.html List of world lights including minor lights with photos.

www.unc.edu/~rowlett/lighthouse/index.htm Comprehensive list of world lights with historic outline, photographs and links.

www.trinityhouse.co.uk Trinity House website with details of all their lighthouses.

www.michaelmillichamp.ukgateway.net England and Wales operational and non-operational lights.

Acknowledgements

Many people have assisted with this book and we are grateful to them all: Vikki Gilson at Trinity House, Martin Garside at the Port of London Authority, Superintendent Coxswain Dave Steenvorden of Humber Lifeboat, Phil Newman of FotoFlite, Peter Bendall, Gerry Douglas-Sherwood and Ruth Drinkwater.

We gratefully acknowledge the people who have supplied images for possible inclusion.

All photographs are by Nicholas Leach, except Tony Denton 14, 15, 16; Trinity House 5 (left), 7 (upper), 12 (lower), 47, 77 (upper), 83; MPL 6, 28, 36; Fotoflite 18, 77 (lower); Klaus Hülse 46, 59, 60, 80; ALK 61 (upper); and Michel Forand 8 (upper) 50, 61 (lower), 71, 88.

Finally, our gratitude extends to Maureen and Sarah for their support and patience during the preparation of this book.

Index